St. Andrews
STORIES FROM THE HOME OF GOLF

The Covers: Front, *Old Course with the ancient Swilcan Bridge in the foreground, detail from a painting by the emerging young Scottish artist Graeme Baxter.* Back, *A player hits towards the road hole, as depicted in another Graeme Baxter painting.* Individual prints of these are available from Baxter Prints, Buchlyvie, Stirlingshire, along with other superb prints of famous courses.

Lang Syne Publishers Ltd.
Strathclyde Business Centre
120 Carstairs Street, Glasgow G40 4JD
Tel: 0141 554 9944 Fax: 0141 554 9955
E-mail: scottishmemories@aol.com
www.langsyneshop.co.uk

Printed by Thomson Litho, East Kilbride

Reminiscences of Golf on St. Andrews Links

by James Balfour-Melville

The following fascinating account of golfing in St. Andrews was first published in 1887 by this prominent Edinburgh lawyer. It is of enormous interest as one of the few first hand accounts of how the course was played in those early days.

HAVING played golf on these Links for somewhere about forty-five years, it has occurred to me to note for my own amusement some of the changes that have taken place during that time in this, one of the most fascinating of all athletic games.

The changes naturally resolve themselves into those on the Links – the Balls – the Clubs.

Before speaking of these, however, it may be well to mark the change of habits in the players during this generation. When I first visited St. Andrews there were only a few resident gentlemen who played, and some occasional strangers from a distance, from Musselburgh, Leith, and Perth. The custom then was to meet in the small Union Parlour in Golf Place about twelve o'clock, and arrange the matches. Parties at once proceeded to play, and if the match was finished two or three holes from home they immediately turned and played their second round, taking a glass of ginger beer at the fourth or "Ginger-beer" Hole. If, however, they finished their first round, they came into the Union Parlour only for ten minutes; did not sit down to lunch but took very slight refreshment, and finished the second round a little after four. The dinner hour was then five.

How different now, when matches are made a week, or even a fortnight, in advance; when places are taken early in the morning, and a man is kept with a record to start each in his turn, and so prevent disputes about the order of play; when play is begun a little after nine, and fifty or sixty matches start between that hour and twelve; when parties have to wait a quarter of an hour for one another at the "high hole"; when an hour or an hour and a half is devoted to lunch, and the second rounds are not begun till between two and half past three! The dinner hour is half-past seven, to give time to have a putting match on the Ladies' Links with the fair and enthusiastic devotees of the game!

The Links belong to Mr. Cheape, the proprietor of the neighbouring estate of Strathyrum. Their length is nearly two miles, and their breadth at the broadest part about 2 2/5ths of a mile. In some distant geological epoch they must have been submerged by the sea, but they are now protected from its waves by high natural embankments of sand. They were originally covered with thick whins, rough grass, heather, and bents. Out of this a golf-course was formed like a narrow ribbon in the form of a shepherd's crook, over which the public have acquired a servitude of playing golf. The course is marked off by march stones. The approximate distance of the holes from one another is as follows: –   Yards

No.	1,	360
"	2,	450
"	3,	335
"	4,	375
"	5,	540
"	6,	370
"	7,	350
"	8,	150
"	9,	300
		3230
		2

1760)6460(3 miles.
5280
1180

Or 3·75 miles.

The length of the course as the crow flies is thus 3·75 miles; but following the ball in a zigzag way, the distance walked is generally considered to be about five miles. The course is marvellously adapted to the game. It used to be flanked by high whins for the greater part of its extent, and these formed an interesting hazard. The turf is smooth and fine; the subsoil is sandy; the surface sometimes undulating and sometimes flat. There are beautiful level putting-greens, while the course is studded with sand-pits, or bunkers, as golfers call them. These, with the ever-recurring hazards of whin, heather, and bent all combine to give endless variety, and to adapt the Links at St. Andrews for the game of golf in a way quite unsurpassed anywhere else. If there be added to its golfing charms the charms of all its surroundings – the grand history of St. Andrews and its sacred memories – its delightful air – the song of its numberless larks, which nestle among the whins – the scream of the sea-birds flying overhead – the blue sea dotted with a few fishing-boats – the noise of its waves – the bay of the Eden as seen from the high hole when the tide is full – the venerable towers and the broken outline of the ancient city; and in the distance the Forfarshire coast, with the range of the Sidlaws, and, further off, the Grampian Hills, it may be truly said that, probably, no portion of ground of the same size on the whole surface of the globe has afforded so much innocent enjoyment to so many people of all ages from two to eighty-nine, and during so many generations.

The changes that have taken place on the course during these forty-five years have been very considerable. First of all, the course is much wider. Formerly there was only one hole on each putting-green and players played to the same hole both going out and coming in. The party first on the green had the right to finish the hole before the match from the opposite direction came up. This naturally kept the course narrow, but when players began to multiply it was found to be inconvenient, and now it would be impossible. To obviate this it was resolved to have two holes on each putting-green, one of them being played to on going out and the other on coming in, or rather there were two distinct putting greens parallel to one another, and a hole in each. This was virtually making two courses all along the Links – one for playing out and the other for coming in; thus the breadth of the course for golfing was gradually increased, till now it is about two-thirds broader than it used to be. This was probably unavoidable, owing to the increased number of players, but it has taken away much of the interest of the game. The only other plan that was suggested was to extend the course round the other side of the Links, and thus make it a circular one; but this was very properly rejected. To that there are many objections. It would have made the course shorter; it would have abolished all the present holes on the homeward line, some of which are so charming in themselves, and full of associations; it would also have deprived parties of the pleasure of meeting their friends, and hearing how their matches were getting on. It is to be hoped that such a proposal will never be renewed.

Let us now consider the changes that have taken place on each of the holes individually, and we shall do so by following the medal round, taking the course out by the right.

1.   The first hole used always to be on the green beside the road. Its hazards were the road across the Links, the burn, the bunker on one side of the putting-green, as well as the turnpike road on the other – making thus a limited green with a narrow approach to it flanked by severe hazards.

The first hole on the medal round now is quite different. It is placed just beyond the burn, on a flat, smooth, broad green to the right of the course. The only hazards in the hole are the road across the Links and the burn. There are none whatever close to the hole.

2.   The tee for the second hole used to be, of course, near the road. There was then no separate teeing-grounds, but the rule was to tee within eight club-lengths of the hole. The ground between the wall and the bunkers towards the corner of the dyke, which is now often preferred as the shortest approach to the hole, was covered with thick whins, and was then quite unplayable. Consequently players were obliged to cross the course, and approach the hole by the right of the bunkers. The whins on the right made the course narrow in that direction, and the low ground to the right of the putting-green could not be played on account of whins and rough grass, so that the hole was much more difficult both in playing and approaching than now. The putting-green, too, which was formerly on a slope, has been made quite level.

At present the tee of this hole is on the right of the Links, while the whins having been driven back, and the low ground to the right near the hole made quite playable, the hole can be played without any bunkers intervening, or any hazards of any kind. Of course if the player goes off the line he has to encounter some hazards. The putting-green, as has been said, is now on a flat and not a slope.

3.   There used to be a thick bank of whins all along the left of the course by the side of the present railway, and the whins and rough grass on the right made it necessary to play straight in the centre, where was the Principal's Nose, with its little satellite of "Tam's Coo" (now filled up). The smaller bunker too, short of these, presented together with them dangerous traps. There was very little room indeed to pass them on either side. The hole was always in *centre of the green,* so that the bunker which crossed the Links beside it had to be played over, else a considerable distance was lost by going to the right or left of it

The tee is now on the right side of the green, and the ball from it is easily played to the right of the Principal's Nose, while the hole being to the right of the putting-green, it is readily approached without crossing the bunker.

4.   Formerly the whins encroached so much on either side that it was necessary that the tee stroke should be played on or over the table in front of the tee, and then a very narrow course was left up to the hole, which was on a narrower putting-green than now, and it was usually placed nearer the bunkers.

The whins having been now driven back, the ball can be played to the right of the table. The course is clear for the second stroke and the hole is placed to the right, far from the bunkers.

5.   This hole is more altered than any other on the Links, and sadly destroyed. The tee stroke used always to be played to the right of the big bunker with the uncouth name, unless when now and then some huge driver "swiped over h – at one immortal go." The second stroke was always to the left on to the Elysian Fields, where the grass was then short and smooth like a putting-green. The third had to navigate the intricate "Beardies," and the fourth was across a wide, staring, horrid bunker, beyond which was a beautiful putting-green. Altogether, this used to be the finest golfing hole, certainly on the Links, and probably in the world. There were beautiful lies when the play was correct, very difficult hazards, and a perfect putting-green.

Now the play is quite different. The Elysian Fields are avoided, and the hole is played on a lower level, where high whins formerly grew, which made play there impossible. There is hardly any hazard; there are no bunkers of any consideration, and the approach to the green is a blind stroke without any bunker between. The hole is altogether much tamer, and less interesting, as well as easier. The young laird of the Links would do the game of golf an unspeakable benefit if he would plough up the low course, or honeycomb it with bunkers, so as to compel players to return to the hole line on the Elysian Fields.

6.   The sixth hole is also much altered. It used to be one of the most dangerous on the Links, but two or three large and important bunkers have been filled up to make a double course. This reduces the number of hazards materially, and the whins have so much disappeared that it is safe to go round the bunkers, playing well to the right, instead of being compelled to play over them. The putting-green, too, is greatly changed. Formerly it had no turf, but was merely earth, heather, and shells, from which it got its name of the heather hole, or the "hole o' shell," but it has now been turfed, and, like the other greens, is carefully kept.

7.   The course here was a narrow one, so that the first stroke was necessarily played over – very often, unfortunately, into – the bunker that crosses the green; but there was not much room to go on either side of it. The putting-green at the high hole, which was always placed near the Eden, was then surrounded with thick, bent grass, leaving a very limited space near the hole. Besides, the ground was sandy and soft. The deterioration of this putting-green has been averted by the growth of rank sea-grass on the banks of the Eden, which prevents the sand from being blown on the Links. These bents were a serious hazard.

8.   The short hole is not much changed, except that the putting-green is wider than it used to be.

9,   or last hole going out, used to be principally heather, but a large portion of that heather was some years ago taken up and relaid with turf. The putting-green is now also much broader than formerly.

Having now reached the end hole, let us retrace our way and compare the holes going home as they now are with what they used to be. This may be thought to be unnecessary, as exactly the same ground has to be travelled over as has been already described. This is quite a mistake. Although the ground is the same, the various holes are as different as if they were on different Links.

1.   The principal difference on the first hole home is that the course was formerly narrower, and the heather has been replaced by turf. If a ball was at all drawn to the left, it used to be either lost in the whins or so imbedded among them that it had to be played out at the sacrifice of at least one stroke, if not more; but now it often lies very tolerably even there, and can be played forward. Near the hole, the ground short of it and to the left was so covered with this grass that if a ball got there it had an exceedingly bad lie. Now the ball has a fair lie where the grass used to be so heavy.

2.   The short hole home is not much changed, except that the bents have disappeared, as already stated, while the putting-green is much harder and broader.

3.   In driving this hole there is now plenty of room to pass the bunker that crossed the green on either side of it. The rough ground at both ends of the putting-green has disappeared, and the putting-green itself has been turfed, and is no longer shelly.

4.   The next hole used to be one of the most difficult on the Links, and more medals have been lost at it than at any other. It has a good many hazards yet, but two of the largest bunkers have been filled up to make a course to the left, as well as one to the right. In former times Allan Robertson used to play the first stroke often with the short spoon short of all the bunkers, and the second with the short spoon over the bunkers, and the third from behind the hill with the short spoon also, on to the green. Now there is plenty of room to avoid the bunkers, both on the right and left: players can have a long stroke off the tee, while long drivers may be on the green in two, and some of the worst bunkers not played over at all.

5.   The long hole home, like the long hole out, has been entirely changed. The big yawning bunker in front of the tee, that was ready to catch a topped ball and to hold it, is almost entirely avoided, while the "Beardies," where so many balls used to be kidnapped, and from which escape was not always made with the loss of only one stroke, are never looked at.

Now the play is on the low ground to the left of the Elysian Fields, thus crossing the bunker diagonally. This line used to be absolutely impossible. There are now no hazards there, or only trifling ones. The hole itself is always placed on the right or left of the putting-green instead of the centre, just between two bunkers the approach to which used to be at the sacrifice of some distance to circumvent the bunkers.

6.   The whins on the left, where the first stroke was played, protruded far on to the Links, and the ball was either caught in them or had to be played right in the centre. There was no possible play to the left of the table, and the second stroke had to go straight over that table; if that stroke were at all short, the ground, which sloped down towards dangerous bunkers, drew the ball into them. Now the hole can be played to the left or right without much risk.

7.   Formerly, there was little room to pass the "Principal's Nose" on either side from the tee, and it, and "Tammy's Coo" beside it, were ugly hazards. The line of whins alongside the present railway was an additional difficulty if the right-hand course was adopted; and if the left, the ground which is now clear was then impracticable from whins. The putting-green itself, as has been mentioned before, has been levelled, so that the hole, instead of being on a slope as formerly, is now on a flat table, and the low ground to the left of it is no longer covered with whins.

8.   Playing off from the hole at the dyke, the ground in front is now cleared of the dense clump of whins that

used to be immediately in front of the tee. There has been no other alteration on this hole of great consequence, except that the grass, which is sometimes long and heavy after much rain, is mowed with a scythe, and a large bank of rushes has been removed.

9.   The principal difference on the last hole is on the putting-green. That has been quite changed by the formation of an artificial table-land, which forms a beautiful green. Formerly the hole was on broken ground in a hollow, with the ground sloping down on both sides. Shortly before my time, there was another serious hazard made by the sea, which came up to the stair of the present Club-House.

That hazard was a very serious one, as the sand at that place was as deep as at the high hole. The last hole being often placed near the edge of the green was close to the sand. But the Links have now been made much wider by the rubbish from the town having reclaimed a large portion from the sea, and there are no hazards on that side.

Having now gone over the golf course both going out and coming in, it only remains further to say on this head that the Links are far more carefully kept than they used to be. Tom Morris superintends this with great assiduity, and he has two men under him who are constantly employed in keeping the bunkers at the proper size, in filling up rabbit-scrapes or other holes, and in returfing places which have given way. The putting-greens also, instead of being left in their natural state as formerly, are now carefully rolled with a heavy roller, – mowed with a machine, – and watered in dry weather from a well that has been sunk near each of them. The putting is made smoother and better, and much truer.

A separate teeing-ground has also been provided at each hole, which preserves the putting-greens from being broken by the tee strokes. A wooden box filled with sand for the tee, and placed at the teeing-ground, is a novelty and an additional refinement.

Changes in balls and clubs and the men who made them

LET us now turn to the changes that have taken place on the Balls. Forty years ago, and indeed from time immemorial, the only kind of ball with which golf had been played was made of leather stuffed with feathers till it was as hard as gutta percha. In making it the leather was cut into three pieces, softened with alum and water, and sewed together by waxed thread, while a small hole was left for putting in the feathers, which was done with a strong stuffing-iron.

The hole in the leather, which did not affect the flight of the ball, but slightly interfered with its putting quality, was then sewed up, and the ball received three coats of paint. A man could make only four balls in a day. They were thus scarce and expensive, and were not round, but rather oblong. The only ball-maker at St. Andrews was Allan Robertson. The trade was hereditary in his family, as both father and grandfather had likewise been ball-makers.

He was assisted by Tom Morris and Lang Willie. They worked together in Allan's kitchen, and the balls were sold at the window at the back of his house, at the corner of the Links and Golf Place. Allan charged 1s 8d. a ball, or £1 a dozen. Gourlay of Musselburgh charged 2s. for each of his. These balls did not last long, perhaps not more than one round. They opened at the seams, especially in wet weather. Indeed, whenever the seam of a ball was cut by the club, the ball burst, and became useless. This very frequently happened, insomuch that the caddies generally took out six or eight balls with them.

About the beginning of the year 1848 balls were first made of gutta percha. I remember the commencement of them perfectly. My brother-in-law, Admiral Maitland Dougall, played a double match at Blackheath with the late Sir Ralph Anstruther and William Adam of Blair-Adam and another friend with gutta-percha balls on a very wet day. They afterwards dined together at Sir Charles Adam's at Greenwich Hospital, and Sir Ralph said after dinner: " A most curious thing – here is a golf ball of gutta percha; Maitland and I have played with it all day in the rain, and it flies better at the end of the day than it did at the beginning." Maitland came to Edinburgh immediately after and told me of this. We at once wrote to London for some of these balls, and went to Musselburgh to try them. Gourlay the ball-maker had heard of them, and followed us around. He was astonished to see how they flew, and being round, how they rolled straight to the hole on the putting-green. He was alarmed for his craft, and having an order from Sir David Baird to send him some balls whenever he had a supply by him, he forwarded to him that evening six dozen! Sir David accordingly was one of the last who adhered to the feather balls, and did not acknowledge the superiority of the others until his large supply was finished. At first they were made with the hand by rolling them on a flat board; thus made, they were round and smooth. They were not painted, but used with their natural brown colour. When new, they did not fly well, but ducked in the air. To remedy this they were hammered with a heavy hammer, but this did not effect the object. They still ducked until they got some rough usage from the check or iron. This made cuts on their sides, which were not liked; but it made them fly. These cuts were easily removed by dipping them in hot water at night. I remember once playing with old Philp, the club-maker (who by the way, was no contemptible player). I had a gutta ball, and he had a feather one. With the dislike which all the tradesmen

then had for the former, he said, "Do you play with these
putty balls?" "Yes," I answered. "But does not the cleek
cut them?" "O yes," I said, "but if you give them a hot
bath at night that puts them all right." "That's the
mischief o't," he replied. Yet it was soon found out that
this same hot bath, while it cured the wound, spoiled the
ball. I remember an amusing proof of this. I and a friend
on the day before the medal played with two guttas, and
they worked beautifully, so that we resolved to play with
them next day for the medal. But as they had been a good
deal hacked, we dipped them in hot water over-night,
and removed these defects. When, however, we played
off the tee next day before an assembled crowd, among
whom were the ball and club-makers, both the balls
whirred and ducked amid the chuckling and jeering and
loud laughter of the onlookers; we had to put down
feather balls next hole. The fact was, they required these
identations to make them fly. About this time it occurred
to an ingenious saddler in South Street to hammer them
all round with the thin or sharp end of the hammer. The
experiment was completely successful, and the ball thus
hammered came rapidly into use, and they were soon
improved by being painted. But the ball-makers were
still bitterly opposed to them, as they threatened to
destroy their trade (no wonder as there were 2456 balls
turned out by Alan Rogbertson in 1844), and both Allan
and Tom resolved that they would never play in a match
where these balls were used. In an unlucky hour, however,
Tom good-naturedly broke his pledge, and played with
a gentleman as his partner who had gutta balls. When
Allan discovered it he was much annoyed with Tom.
Tom, when he saw this, gave up his employment under
him, and opened a shop of his own, where he made both
kinds of balls, and also clubs. Allan in a little time
followed suit with the balls, as he discovered that he
could make a dozen guttas in a shorter time than he could
make one feather ball, and the sale of them increased

prodigiously. After that an iron mould was invented for making these balls, and on being taken from the mould, they were indented with the thin end of the hammer. But latterly the moulds have the indentations in them, so that the ball is now produced indented and ready for being painted. The balls are made everywhere now, but some are better than others, probably because the maker takes greater pains to use good gutta percha.

Various modifications of this ball have been tried, but without success. Lately, however, another kind has been played with, called the *Eclipse*. It is not exactly known how it is made, but it is supposed to be a composition of gutta percha and vulcanised india-rubber and cork. It is a little softer than the gutta-percha ball, it makes no click when struck by the club, while the irons make no mark on it, nor does it ever lose its shape. It is a moot point whether it or the gutta-percha ball is the best, and some of the finest players differ as to that. The professionals generally prefer the gutta. Those who like the Eclipse claim for it that it holds the wind better; it runs better, especially if the ground is hard either from frost or drought; and they think it is more to be depended on in putting. On the other hand, those who prefer the guttas say that, if they do not run so far as the others, they fly further; that they require less physical force, as they spring with greater elasticity from the club; that they are more easily picked up and dropped near the hole at the approach stroke. They maintain, too, that they putt as well as the others, and they like to hear the click in striking, to which they have been accustomed. But whatever be the comparative merits of the two balls, it is not improbable that the Eclipse will be the ball of the future, unless something else is invented. They last much longer, and so are a good deal cheaper than the guttas. For this reason boys naturally play with them. They will get accustomed to them in their youth, and will continue with them when they become men.

The change in the Clubs has not been so important as on the Balls, but some have been discontinued that were formerly used, and others have been introduced. For example, the driving putter is never now played with. It was a club with a putter head, but with a flatter angle than a putter, a shaft about the length of a middle spoon, and though stiff, had a spring in it. It was used to play out of bents and thick grass, but as these have now disappeared, so has the club. It was convenient, too, for playing against the wind.

Another club that I fear is fast getting obsolete is the Baffing Spoon. As golfers know, to baff a ball is to touch the turn below the ball pretty firmly when it is struck, and the ball is thus raised into the air. The Baffy is a very short spoon, about the length of a putter, but spooned twice the depth of an ordinary short spoon. It is used when near the hole, and when the ball has to be lifted over a hazard or uneven ground. There are few prettier strokes in the game. The ball is tossed high in the air, and hovers for a moment, as if to choose what blade of grass to alight on, then drops, and does not run above a foot or so. It is not only a pretty stroke, but a very effective one when well played. In the hands of Captain Dalgleish, Sir David Baird, Shihallion, or Sir Robert Hay, the Baffy was a wonderful weapon. But now men have grown so fond of cleeks and irons in all shapes and sizes that it is despised. It is said that Allan Robertson introduced the use of the cleek when near the hole. If so, it is, I think, a pity that he did. It is not so pretty a stroke; it destroys the green, as some even intentionally cut the turf with it; and it is not more sure than the stroke with the "Baffy."

While these two clubs have gone out of fashion, two others have been introduced. One is the Iron Niblick, with which to play out of bunkers, or when in a hole or cart-rut. It is a heavy iron, with a short round head, and is admirably adapted for bunkers, as it takes much less sand than the ordinary heavy iron with which that stroke used to be played.

The other new club is the Wooden Niblick. It is a long spoon, with a very short head, plated with brass on the bottom, from which it gets its other name of the "Brassy." It is used for playing a cupped or bad-lying ball, or a ball on a road. On a road the brass bottom saves the club from being destroyed by the hard metal, or turned so easily as a wooden one would be. It is extremely useful, and with its short head many men can play a cupped ball as well as a ball from the tee with a play-club. No set would be complete without having both an Iron Niblick and a Brassy.

The first prize – a Silver Club

The first prize played for by the Club was a silver club, the winner of which was to be Captain for the year, and was to attach to it a silver ball, with his name and the date of his having won the club. It was first played for in 1754, and has been regularly the Captain's prize ever since, so that it is now covered with medals. These are treated with great reverence, as all new members are required to kiss them at the first dinner which he attends after his election.

This prize was competed for in the ordinary way for many years; but by and by the Club came to be of opinion that the Captain, instead of being only distinguished as a first-class golfer, should rather be a gentleman of good social position who took an interest in the game, his principal duties being to preside at the dinners and ball, and to represent the Club in society. It was accordingly agreed that, while he should be Captain by virtue of winning the silver club, some one should be selected by the old Captains, against whom no other member should play. The plan has been long acted on, the gentleman selected playing only one stroke, when he is declared winner of the club.

In 1833 Mr. Whyte-Melville presented the Club with a silver putter, on the understanding that, although no balls were to be appended to it, the gold medals of the Club should be attached, so that, as the silver club handed down to posterity the names of those who had presided over its meetings, the putter might transmit in a similar manner the medals bearing the names of those members who had signalised themselves by their superiority at play in the game of golf.

On the system of selection, a great number of noblemen and gentlemen have been Captains. In the year 1864 the Prince of Wales was nominated as Captain, but as His Royal Highness could not be present, both his play and duties as Captain were done by proxy. But in 1875 the late Prince Leopold, Duke of Albany, was selected, and he was good enough to come to St. Andrews for the purpose. There was great excitement in the prospect of his visit. The day before the medal was wet and gloomy, but immediately after breakfast on the medal day it cleared up, and the weather became charming. The Prince stayed at Mount Melville. While driving in the morning, he saw St. Andrews bright with flags at every available place – so bright that the ancient city hardly knew itself. On appearing on the Links, a great concourse of spectators had assembled to see High Royal Highness play for the club. A rope was stretched out to prevent the people from crowding upon him. Tom Morris teed his ball, and the Prince, evidently a little nervous lest he should top it, struck a good, clean, long stroke over the heads of the people, amid much cheering. He was then declared winner of the club, which was proclaimed, as usual, by the firing of the cannon. The gold medals were afterwards competed for, forty-seven couples joining in the contest. His Royal Highness followed some of the favourite players, and watched the game. In the evening he presided at the dinner, where he presented the medals with his usual gracious and affable manner. He also gave a handsome silver medal of his own to the winner of William the Fourth's medal, to be retained by him as a memorial of his being Captain. He presided at the ball next evening, when, by his whole bearing there, as well as during all his visit to St. Andrews, he won the hearts of every one. Nowhere were the tidings of his early death in 1884 received with more real sorrow.

It may be mentioned that the uniform worn by the Captain in the evening, both at the dinner and ball, as well as the former Captains, is a red dress coat, with blue collar, and gilt buttons, stamped with a St. Andrew's cross. The uniform of the members of the Club on the Links is a red jacket, with blue collar, and gilt buttons with the St. Andrew's cross. At one time it was compulsory on members to wear their uniform when playing, under penalty of a fine. But when it became customary for gentlemen to wear shooting-coats in the forenoon, the rule was not enforced, and the uniform is now not always used.

After the arrangement by which the Captain was to be virtually elected, the Club gave a gold medal, to be competed for once a year. It was to be gained by the member who did a round of the Links in the fewest number of strokes. Any two members can play against each other as they may arrange, and the order in which they start is fixed by ballot on the previous day. This medal was first played for in 1806, and it continued to be the principal golfing prize until the year 1837, when His Majesty King William the Fourth – who had in 1834 become patron of the Club, and authorised it to be styled "The Royal and Ancient Golf Club of St. Andrews" – presented the Club with a handsome gold medal, to be played for annually. This medal from that year became the first prize of the Club, and the second was the Club gold medal. They are both competed for on the same day in autumn – generally the last Wednesday of September.

In 1838 the Queen-Dowager graciously presented the Club with a gold medal, called the Royal Adelaide Medal, which was to be worn by the Captain during his term of office.

Besides these gold medals, Major Belches of Invermay in 1836 presented the Club with a "silver cross of St. Andrew's;" and in 1846 the Bombay Club presented it with a silver medal. These silver prizes are competed for at the spring meeting of the Club – generally on the first Wednesday of May – on the same terms and in the same way as the other prizes are played for in autumn.

In 1881 the Royal Blackheath Golf Club presented to the Royal and Ancient Golf Club of St. Andrews a gold medal, in honour of Mr. George Glennie, who was a respected member of both Clubs. It is competed for both in May and October, and is gained by the player whose combined scores at the spring and autumn meetings are the lowest.

The only handicap prize in the Club is a handsome cup, which was presented by the Calcutta Golf Club, and was played for in 1885 for the first time. It is decided, not by strokes, but by holes, the various players receiving odds from those that are fixed as scratch.

Captain Daniel Stewart, the Captain of the Club for last year (1886), presented a silver jug to the player who should do the last nine holes when playing for the medal in the fewest strokes, and who should not gain either of the medals. The idea was that any player who had been unfortunate in going out might be encouraged still to keep up his interest in the game to the close. The jug was not a challenge prize, but was to be retained by the winner.

All these prizes, except Prince Albert's and Captain Stewart's, are challenge prizes, to be held only for a year; but the winners of the gold medals in autumn and the silver prizes in spring each receive a small medal, in gold and silver respectively, to be retained by them, and worn on the coat.

Happy days on the Links

Now let me indulge myself by recalling the memory of some of those who are gone, with whom I have often played. Among all the great variety of persons with whom I have joined the game, Sir Hope Grant was my most constant opponent. He was a charming companion and fast friend, a perfect gentleman both in feeling and manner, a distinguished and eminent soldier, a graceful rider, and an excellent player on the violoncello, of which he was passionately fond. He was also one of the keenest golfers I ever knew, and I have known few who played better. He drove long, low balls, held his cleek short, played it from the knee, and when he was in form was a very good putter, always using a wooden club, which he held short. I first met him in 1851, when he came home from the first Chinese war, and before the Indian Mutiny, where he distinguished himself so gallantly. His friends crowded round him at the Union Parlour. They knew what a fine player he had been, and that he used to play matches for £100 with John Wood, the best gentlemen player then, or perhaps that ever was, at Musselburgh. A match was made up for him, in which I happened to be one of the players. Before starting, Sir Hugh Playfair, who was not playing, said, "You know, Hope, that I don't bet much, but I will go half a sovereign on this match with you." Sir Hugh did not know what an entire change had come over Sir Hope's religious principles during his residence in India and China, and which involved a change of practice; but Sir Hope (or Colonel Grant, as he then was) at once answered, "Oh, I forgot to tell you all that I have given up that sort of thing, and I now play for

nothing." "Go half a crown," said Sir Hugh. "No, nothing."
"A something – a fiddle-string." "No, nothing." He was
delighted to find that I acted on the same principle, and
never betted, believing that the game in itself is sufficiently
interesting without adding to it the gambler's excitement.
From that hour began a fast friendship between us, which
never had a check till he died in 1875. When he died Sir
Stafford Northcote said of him very truly in the House of
Commons, of which he was then the leader, "His modesty
was equal to his courage." And there were his two
brothers – John Grant of Kilgraston, and Sir Francis,
President of the Royal Academy. They were not great
golfers, but very fond of it, and were both excellent
company. Sir Hugh Playfair's name will be long
remembered and his influence felt in St. Andrews. He
inaugurated the Union Parlour, where the entry-money
was £1 and the annual subscription 5s. He also
commenced the present Club House, which has grown
into such comfortable proportions. The entry-money is
now £8, and the annual subscription £3. The membership
is 870. Then there was his brother-in-law, Captain Archie
Dalgleish, once the cock of the green. These two used to
take up all strangers coming to St. Andrews, and were
seldom beaten. There was also Captain Campbell,
familiarly called Shihallion, and Saddell (another
Campbell), magnificent and pompous, and Sir Thomas
Moncrieffe, with a lively, pleasing manner; Sir Robert
Hay, who was tall and handsome, with an elegant style
of play; Sir Ralph Anstruther and his brother, afterwards
Colonel Lloyd Anstruther, with the former's popular son
Sir Robert, and George Whyte-Melville the novelist –
witty, agreeable, and kindly, full of racy anecdotes in the
Club between rounds; George Glennie, who was never
excelled at any part of the game by a gentleman player,
and whose modest bearing made him universally liked.
Then there was Sir John Low of Clatto, who long held
high appointments in India, and whose manners were

cultured by associating with princes and statesmen; his excellent brother, the Colonel; my old schoolfellow, Goddard, whose beautiful style was modelled on that of John H. Wood, of whom it has been said that it was a study in the fine arts to see John Wood strike a ball. There was also J. O. Fairlie of Coodham, well known on the race-course and in the hunting field, but a keen golfer, and a first-class player. Having learned the game rather late in life, his style was not graceful. He played with his whole body rather than with his arms, but he drove well, and was very sure. His manner was quiet and still; when playing important matches he was always silent. I once tied with him for William the Fourth's medal, and in playing off the tie he never uttered a single word during the whole round, not even in answer to an observation.

There are others yet alive, whom I forbear to name, but I must not forget my dear old relative, Mr. Whyte-Melville, who, while he never was a fine player, was a capital partner, and was extremely fond of the game, and who played till he was just past eighty-five – three days every week, and two rounds every day, in summer and winter, and in all weathers – wind, rain, snow or sunshine. On his death-bed he asked me to take a set of his clubs as a memorial of the many pleasant matches we had had together. I felt it to be kind and touching. He was deservedly popular. He and Lady Catherine dispensed profuse hospitality at their family seat of Mount Melville, about three miles from St. Andrews. When he was about 77, the Club asked him to allow his picture to be painted, that it might be placed in the Club House. It is a full-length portrait, by his old friend Frank Grant – one of the last and one of the best of his portraits. It is not only a good likeness, but an excellent golfing picture. He is represented as having finished the first hole at the road going out. His putter is still in his hand. His caddie is teeing his ball, while his play club is lying on the ground ready to be handed to him. The ancient stone bridge over the burn is shown – once the only bridge across the burn, and which has been traversed homeward by many an anxious foot when the match was all even and one to play; the Club House is in the distance, with the Martyrs' Monument. The only other portrait in the Club is that of Sir Hugh Playfair.

The late Lord Eglinton was a keen player at this, as at most other athletic sports. He was at St. Andrews in October 1861, and on the day before the medal the weather was beautiful. He played three rounds with Mr. Grant of Kilgraston, Sir Francis Grant, and Mr. Little Gilmour. After Sir Hope and I had finished our match, he asked me to go out a few holes and walk in with his brothers and Lord Eglinton. We did so; his lordship was enjoying himself extremely. He expressed his delight with the scenery at the high hole – and indeed he frequently admired the whole landscape, as the descending sun lengthened our shadows on that October afternoon. He afterwards went out to Mount Melville to dinner. When coming away in the evening he complained to a friend, as they were passing through the library, that he had felt rather unwell in the drawing-room, but that he was all right. When, however, he got to the hall, while the butler was helping him on with his great-coat, he fell down in a fit of apoplexy, was carried to a bedroom, never spoke again, and died two days after. As may be supposed, this cast a sad gloom over the gathering for the medal next day, all the more that on the same day another well-known member of the Club, Mr. Guthrie of Craigie, had a stroke of apoplexy in the billiard-room; but he recovered, and lived for some years.

Mr. Stuart Grace, though not himself a golfer, having been the indefatigable Secretary of the Club since 1842 till 1885 – that is, ever since I was a member of it, – I must not omit to mention. It is rather remarkable that four generations of Mr. Grace's family have been Secretaries of the Club. His grandfather was Secretary for thirty years; his father for twenty-four years, and himself for forty-three years; his son has now been elected as his successor. The three first members of the family were honorary Secretaries. At the close of the late Mr. Grace's tenure of office, the Club presented him with a service of plate; Mr. Stuart Grace, who has recently retired, has also been presented with silver plate, which he has well deserved for the attention which he has paid to the business of the Club for so long a period, and for the courtesy which he has invariably shown to all its members.

Why Tom Morris refused to take the winning bet

Of club-makers, no man has ever approached Hugh Philp, and even now to possess a club of his, is a treasure like an old Cremona violin to a musician, or a Toledo blade to a swordsman. He was a quiet and thoroughly respectable man, had a fine eye for a club, with exquisite taste, while he was simple and natural in his manner. His assistant, James Wilson, who worked with him for many years, and after his death opened an establishment of his own, was also much liked.

Let me recall some of the professionals and the old caddies. First among these was Allan Robertson, the prince of golfers. He and his father and grandfather had been ball-makers, when feather balls were the only balls, for more than a hundred years. He was a short, little, active man, with a pleasant face, small features, and a merry twinkle in his eye. He was universally popular, not a bit forward, but withal easy and full of self-respect. He generally wore a red, round jacket, and played constantly with gentlemen, both in matches of great importance, and in those that were only more or less important. His style was neat and effective. He held his clubs near the end of the handle, even his putter high up. His clubs were light, and his stroke an easy, swift switch. With him the game was one as much of head as of hand. He always kept cool, and generally pulled through a match even when he got behind. He was a natural gentleman, honourable and true. He died of jaundice on 1st September 1859, when only about the age of forty-four, much regretted.

Next to him was Tom Morris, now called "Old Tom". He began by helping Allan to make balls, and was very nearly his match at the game. His style I need not describe, as all golfers of the present generation know it. He still flourishes on the Links, and is still a fine player. He and Allan were together the champions of their day. Tom has always been respected, not only as a player, but for his excellent private character. There is an anecdote told of him which I have great pleasure in repeating, because it is so honourable to him. On one occasion he was playing with the late Captain Broughton, and when at the high hole Tom's ball was lying in the bents that used then to surround it, the Captain said, "O Tom, you had better give up the hole; you are playing three more, and you are in the bents." "No," said Tom; "I'll perhaps hole this." "I'll give you £50 if you do." "Done with you, Captain," said Tom, and he holed it! Next morning the Captain brought £50, and handed it to him. "What is that?" said Tom. "What you won yesterday." "Take it away," exclaimed Tom, "I would not touch it. We were both in fun." This was exceedingly creditable to Tom, and showed real good feeling. If he had taken it, no one could have found fault with him, and £50 offered to a tradesman was a temptation. I had often heard the story from Campbell of Saddell, who was present, and other gentlemen, but I once asked Tom himself about it. He said it was all true, and he laughingly added, "You should have seen the Captain's face when I went in!" Tom, as is well known, is now the Conservator of the Links, and has a large establishment for making both clubs and balls.

His son, "Young Tommy," was perhaps the best player that ever appeared on the green. He was a tall, handsome athlete, and unmatched at all parts of the game. His victorious career began in 1867, when he was sixteen. It continued without a break till his early death in 1875. During these eight years he exhibited as remarkable a display of golf as has ever been seen. When he died, at the early age of twenty-four, he was buried in the ground at the old Cathedral, where a monument has been erected to his memory by contributions from sixty golfing clubs.

Among the older professionals were the twin brothers Dunn of Musselburgh. They were beautiful golfers, and fought many pitched battles with Allan and Tom. They ran them hard, but could not beat them .

Referring to the caddies, there were Sandy Pirip, who carried for Sir Hope Grant, and Sandy Herd, who carried first for Saddell and afterwards for Mr. Whyte-Melville; Charlie Thomson, once a crack player, as most of the others were; and many other most respectable men. But perhaps the greatest character among them was "Lang Willie." He was very tall, about six feet two, with bent knees and a slouching gait, a tall hat, swallow-tailed blue coat, and light trousers. His look was rather stupid, but he was in reality wide awake. He used to insist that he drank nothing but sweet milk, greatly to Allan's amusement, who knew better. He was much taken out as an instructor of beginners, and when one met him and asked him how his pupil was getting on, he had always the same stereotyped answer, "Jist surprisin'," which might mean either very well or very ill. On one occasion he was teaching one of the Professors of the university the noble game. But the said Professor was not a promising pupil. As he hammered away, sometimes "missing the globe," sometimes topping the ball, or cutting up large divots of turf, Willie fairly got out of patience, and said to him, "You see, Professor, as long as ye are learning thae lads at College Latin and Greek it is easy work, but when ye come to play golf ye maun hae a heid!" On another occasion he was carrying in a match, when, at the last hole coming home, the party had to wait till a young man on horseback had passed along the road. The rider was not very steady in his saddle, and Willie quietly remarked, "I think that lad is a wee lowse in the glue" – a phrase which golfers will understand who have felt the inconvenience of their club-head getting rather loose. Willie had more than one stroke of paralysis. I could not help being amused at his description of the first one. I asked him one day what he had felt. He said he felt nothing but in the morning his sister said to him that his face was twisted. "I said to her, 'Nonsense, lassie,' but when I sat down to my parritch my jaw wouldna work!" At last he was overtaken by a fit on the Links, was carried home in an omnibus, and died about twenty minutes after.

Stuffed swallow mounted on the ball that killed it!

From what has been said as to the changes in the Links, the Balls, and the Clubs, it is obvious that the round ought to be done in much fewer strokes now than formerly. How many fewer it is not easy to determine accurately . Some say twenty. I incline to think fifteen or sixteen, but I believe that every year it will be done in fewer for some little time, as the course gets broader and the hazards fewer. The best gauge, perhaps, is the score at which the medal has been gained from time to time. In 1834 it was taken at 97 by Mr. Robert Oliphant; 1839 Mr. Andrew Stirling and Mr. John H. Wood of Leith tied for it at 99; but these were exceptionally low; at that time it was reckoned to be very good if the medal was won at 103 or 104.

The fall has since been graduated, thus proving that is is not so much, at least, the superiority of the players now, but the comparative ease of the game. Young players are apt to think that the play is superior to what it used to be, but old men doubt this. They admit that the first-class players are more numerous than they formerly were, but they think that is because the game is played by a greater number. The proportion is probably nearly the same.

After the introduction of gutta-percha balls, but before the change of the greens, the numbers fell to 98, 97, 96, at which last figure the silver cross was gained in the spring of 1850 by Mr. George Condie, and in 1852 Captain Maitland Dougall, and in 1853 Mr. Jelf Sharpe, each gained the same prize at the same figure – 96. But the autumn medal had never been gained under 97. I have a vivid recollection of the autumn of the year 1850, when King William the Fourth's medal was played for. The Club was then just a hundred years old. The late Earl of Eglinton was Captain. There was a large turn-out both of players and spectators; most, if not all, of the best players of the day were present. The weather was lovely. One of the most successful medal-players of his time, now Admiral Maitland Dougall, who had gained the silver cross at 96 the year before, came in early in the day at 95, and was congratulated by every one on being sure to be the winner, and at a stroke lower than any medal had ever been gained during a hundred years before. But a little later in the day I was fortunate enough to come in at 93, and still later to my mortification, Captain Stewart came in in 90, he thus winning the first medal, and I the second. It may be interesting to see some of the scores on that day. They were as follows:-

Captain Stewart 90
Mr. Balfour......................................93
Captain Maitland Dougall.....................95
Mr. George Condie 96
Mr. Goddard 96
Mr. Glennie 96
Mr. P. Alexander 99
Mr. Campbell of Saddel 100
Mr. Ord Campbell 100
Mr. Thomas Moncrieffe 102

Bets were taken that the medals would never be won in 90 and 93 again. But they were. Shortly after the double holes with the double course were introduced, when the score began to fall more decidedly, insomuch that in the spring of 1883 the silver cross was gained by Mr. Alexander Stuart at 83, the lowest that it has yet reached, and in the autumn of 1886 King William the Fourth's medal was gained by Mr. S. M. Ferguson at 84, the lowest score for that medal.

Looking over the list of medal-holders, it will be observed that in the history of the Club the first gold medal has been gained for three years in succession by only two members, viz., Mr. Robert Patullo in 1812- 12-14, and Mr. Leslie M. Balfour in 1875-76-77. Mr. George Glennie gained the King William the Fourth medal in 1855, at 88, before there were double holes, a figure which was never equalled till 1879, twenty-four years afterwards, when Mr. Charles Anderson gained it also at 88, but on a very different kind of green; and in spring of that same year Mr. W. J. Mure gained the silver cross at 86.

It is very pleasant to recall matches, or even special strokes or singular incidents, that will not occur twice in a lifetime, of which all golfers have so many. For example, the Lord Justice-Clerk (Lord Moncrieff) once told me that when he was playing a match with Lord Rutherfurd Clark, Mr. Donald Crawford, M.P., and Mr. Patrick Blair,

W.S., his opponent's (Mr. Crawford) ball lay between 80 and 90 yards from the hole; the stick with the flag happened not to be quite in the hole, as it ought to have been, but about a foot from it. Crawford played with his cleek, struck the stick, and holed his ball. Lord Moncreiff played next, and performed exactly the same feat. He was a yard or two nearer. He also played with his cleek, struck the stick, and went in, thus halving the hole. According to the doctrine of chances, how unlikely this was! It may be mentioned, as a singular coincidence, that at the same hole, the week after, the Lord Justice-General, the chief of the other division of the Court of Session, holed his ball from about the same lace off his short spoon, the Fates thus showing their impartiality by dealing their chances equally to both judges.

Again, I once, but only once, saw a long stroke played with the long spoon, and carry, not roll, into the hole, and remain there.

Another singular incident occurred when on one occasion I was playing against Sir Hope Grant. We were going to the high hole coming home. Allan Robertson happened to be at the hole, and held up the stick. Sir Hope struck first, and went into the hole in one, on which Allan flung the flag into the air. I said, "Come, I have this for the half," and played. I went about a foot from the hole, and easily holed in two. I would have given a good deal to halve it in one; but there is no record of this ever having been done, and probably it never will be. We all know that the short hole has been occasionally done in one, but I have never heard of any other instance in which it was lost in two.

I have played many exciting matches which I have forgotten all about, but one or two I have not forgotten. One I especially remember, having recorded it at the time. It was played on 24th and 25th August 1863, between George Condie and his brother-in-law, Major Boothby, against Mr. Hodge and myself. We were all then

ST. ANDREWS — The R. & A. from Swilcan Burn

The ruined St. Andrews Castle dating from the thirteenth century

The Old Course covered in a winter bla

— another painting by Graeme Baxter.

View towards the 18th hole at St. Andrews Golf Course.

The university town of St. Andrews, seen from the 108 foot tower of St. Rule in the ruined cathedral.

in the zenith of our game, and George Condie was as fine a gentleman player as was ever on the Links. We played for two days-three rounds the first day, and three rounds and a half the second, or 113 holes in all; and at the end of the 112th we were all even! Condie and Boothby gained the last hole.

A match that created a good deal of interest at the time arose from a challenge which appeared in the Field newspaper, from a father and son at Westward Ho, to play any other father and son in the country, the match to be three rounds of St. Andrews Links, on two consecutive days. My son Leslie and I accepted the challenge. The match was played on the 10th and 12th October 1874, in presence of a large gallery, and we had the satisfaction of beating them by seven holes.

A curious circumstance which happened to Major Chiene may be noticed. On one occasion when he was playing his ball accidentally struck a swallow when on the wing, and killed it. The Major had the bird stuffed, and set upon the identical ball that killed it; it was placed as a curiosity in the Clubroom, where it remained for many years.

Among the variety of incidents that have accompanied the play for the medal was one which occurred in 1860, when an extraordinary tempest raged. The wind from the north was howling, and the rain lashing. Just as parties were about to start a cry was heard that a vessel was being wrecked in the offing. The play for the medal was postponed. The lifeboat was launched; but there was great difficulty in getting it manned. Maitland Dougall, who was about to play, when he heard of the difficulty, volunteered to go, and took the stroke oar. The men were rescued, and the lifeboat came ashore in the afternoon. The play for the medal was begun after the arrival of the lifeboat. The wind was still furious. It was to Maitland Dougall's credit that, though his arms were sore, and he was stiff and all wet, he gained the Club gold medal at

112 strokes. Gourlay, the Musselburgh ball-maker, who was present, remarked, "What nerve the Captain must have for the game!" that he (Gourlay) would not have gone out in that boat for a thousand pounds.

A peculiar experience I myself once had in playing for the medal. I stood lowest for the Club gold medal, and Mr. Robert Clark, in playing the last hole home, lay near the road at one stroke fewer than I was. He played a pretty long stroke with his cleek, and actually *holed his ball,* thus tying with me for the medal! He gained the tie.

St. Andrews becomes the Mecca of Golf

During the course of these years the character of the game is a good deal altered. It happened that, coincident with the introduction of gutta-percha balls, a railway was opened through Fife, with a station at Leuchars, six miles from St. Andrews, from whence there was a service of omnibuses, and in a year or two afterwards a branch line was formed. This made St. Andrews, which had hitherto been rather a retired place of learned and ecclesiastical leisure, much more accessible. The consequence was that houses and villas quickly sprang up. Together, these influences had the effect of somewhat destroying the patrician and rather exclusive tone of the game. They so popularised it as to make it a game for all classes; and all classes do play at it-judges of the Supreme Court, officers of high rank in the Army and Navy, noblemen, tradesmen, men of all professions and of all ages, fathers and sons. I have seen a match played, the aggregate age of the players in which was 323.

Nor is it in Scotland alone that the game is now played, but in many parts of England, where there are players that are quite first-class; in India and Canada also, and almost all the Colonies. A few years ago I followed a match that was being played on the famous heights of Abraham at Quebec.

Wherein do the charms of this game lie, that captivate youth, and retain their hold till far on in life? I have known the game survive all other sports – football, cricket, shooting, salmon-fishing, hunting and deer-stalking. Probably it owes much to the variety of its attractions. It is a fine, open air, athletic exercise, not violent, but bringing into play nearly all the muscles of the body; while that exercise can be continued for hours. But it would be a mistake to suppose that it is only muscular exertion that is required. It is a game of skill, needing mind and thought and judgement, as well as a cunning hand. It is also a social game, where one may go out with one friend or with three, as the case may be, and enjoy mutual intercourse, mingled with an excitement which is very pleasing, while it never requires to be associated with the degrading vice of gambling. It never palls or grows stale, as morning by morning the players appear at the teeing-ground with as keen a relish as if they had not seen a club for a month. Nor is it only while the game lasts that its zest is felt. How the player loves to recall the strokes and other incidents of the match, so that it is often played over again next morning while he is still in bed! But even more does it absorb the conversation of the evening. The late George Hughes wrote to his brother, the author of *Tom Brown's School-days*, trying to convert him to "Golfomania," as he called it; and speaking of the after-dinner conversation about the game, he says: "The humour of the whole thing was positively sublime. You have heard squires at their wine after a good run; bless you, they can't hold a candle to golfers. Most of the players were Scotch, and the earnestness with which the Scotch 'play' is a caution." This is true. How in the evening each dilates on his own wonderful strokes, and the singular chances that befell him in the different parts of the green! – all under the pleasurable delusion that every listener is as interested in his game as he himself is. How he tells of his long swipes, which he is not sure have ever been equalled, and of the perfect pitch which he made with the barry, or iron, at the approach stroke, just carrying the bunker that intervened, and narrowly escaping the whins on the left! And then the long putt – how beautifully the ball rolled over the smooth green up to the very lip of the hole, or, more fortunate still, dropped into it! What putts! I remember Saddell once saying, as he looked at a fine putt that borrowed a little from the side of the undulating ground, and dribbled gently down, down, down into the hole, "What a splendid putt! In my time I have had the best grouse-shooting in Scotland, and the best salmon river, and the best deer-stalking, and I have kept the best hunters at Melton; but I am thankful to say I can now dream about a putt!"

But I must close these reminiscences. To recall such memories has been both pleasant and pathetic – pleasant because they have brought back the sunny hours of recreation in a busy and happy life; pathetic, because they have been associated with so many who are now gone. How quickly these forty-five years have receded into the past! and now, looking back on them, one naturally sympathises with the Roman poet when he says:

Eheu! fugaces, Posthume, Posthume,
Labuntur anni.

St. Andrews Golfing Diary

1457. Scottish Parliament bans golf and insists the people play archery instead.King James 11 says the love of golf and neglect of target practise is endangering the nation's defences!

1552. First written record of golf in St. Andrews when Archbishop John Hamilton is given a document which safeguards the rights of citizens to play on the links without hindrance.

1598. The Kirk is not amused by citizens who are out golfing when they should be at morning service!

1618. The "featherie" ball is introduced.

1691. Firmly on the map, St. Andrews is described as the "Metropolis of Golfing".

1754. On May 14 the Society of St. Andrews Golfers, forerunner of the Royal and Ancient Club, is founded because the town is the "Alma Mater of Golf". "Twenty-two Noblemen and Gentlemen being admirers of the ancient and healthful exercise of the Golf" met to draft certain articles and laws to form the Society. They certainly started something for the R and A is now the best known organisation on the world golfing stage today.

1764. The first introduction of 18 holes followed 13 years later by the first rules for tee-ing.

1797. The town council sells the links.

1821. The first survey of the Old Course is carried out.

1832. The Greens are doubled in size to speed up play.

1834. The Society of Golfers changes its name to the "Royal and Ancient Golf Club".

1836. The longest featherie drive is recorded — 361 yards.

1838. The first rule for lost ball penalty is introduced.

1845. The R and A stop the trains! A railway was to be built cutting through the Links at Burn Hole but our golfing guardians successfully applied to have it rerouted.

1848. The first gutta balls go on sale.

1854. The Royal and Ancient Clubhouse, now a famous landmark known to golfers throughout the world, was built.

1857. A foursomes event becomes the first championship played at St. Andrews.

1858. Allan Robertson is the first professional and the first man to break 80. The first steward at a golf match also made his appearance in this year.

1860. The Open Championship is established.

1865. Tom Morris is appointed first professional of the R and A.

1867. First Ladies' Club formed.

1870. "Young Tom" Morris wins his third successive Open in a row.

1872. Tom is first again and is presented with the New Trophy.

1873. The first Open is played at St. Andrews.

1874. The Town Council want to take part of the links for building but a successful legal action stops them.

1875. Young Tom Morris dies at just 24 and the town is in mourning.

1888. The R and A issue Rules of Golf to all golf clubs, three years after being approached to form an Association under one set of rules.

1893. Willie Auchterlonie is winner of the Open.

1894. Townspeople win back the links and Parliament lays down arrangements with the R and A. Also in this year the winner of the Open receives £40. The 1990 first prize was £85,000. How times have changed!

1895. The New Course is opened.

1897. The Jubilee Course is built by the Town Council to mark Queen Victoria's Diamond Jubilee.

1902. Sandy Herd wins the Open using the Haskell Rubber Ball. The New Golf Club is founded.

1908. Tom Morris dies.

1912. Green fees are introduced for visitors.

1914. In the year the First World War broke out, the Eden Course is opened.

1919. The war is over, and the R and A takes over the management of British Championships.

1921. The Open trophy goes to America for the first time when it is won by Jock Hutchison, a superb player who was born in St. Andrews but later emigrated with his family.

1929. The R and A legalise steel shafts in Britain.

1930. Bobby Jones wins the Amateur on the Old Course as part of his "Grand Slam".

1933. Spectators are charged gate money for the first time.

1946. St. Andrews rate-payers have to start paying for their golf. Crowd control is introduced for matches.

1950. Australia win the First Commonwealth Tourna–
       ment. Also in this year the R and A and United
       States Golf Association agree to meet from time
       to time and review a uniform, world-wide code of
       conduct which the major golfing countries had
       drawn up for the game.

1955. The Open is shown on television for the first time.

1958. Bobby Jones is given a great honour — he is
       made a Freeman of St. Andrews.

1960. Centenary Open Championship is played at St.
       Andrews.

1967. Alcan World Championship, the world's biggest
       money tournament, is inaugurated on the Old
       Course.

1968. The Laurie Auchterlonie Golf Museum and the
       Old Course Hotel are both opened in this year.

1970. Jack Nicklaus wins the Open after a play-off with
       Doug Sanders.

1971. Bobby Jones dies. Ground at Balgrove is bought
       for a beginners' course.

1972. The Tenth Hole is dedicated to Bobby Jones. The
       Bing Crosby Tournament is inaugurated. The
       Balgove course is opened.

1978. Fairway watering is installed on the Old Course.
       Jack Nicklaus wins the Open.

1980. Rusack's Hotel is sold to the Links Trust.

1982. The Old Course Hotel is sold to Mr. Frank
       Sheridan.

1983. Princess Anne formally opens the Old Course
       Golf and Country Club. The links Changing Rooms
       Complex opens in the lower ground floor of
       Rusack's Hotel.

1984   Jack Nicklaus receives honorary degree from University. Severiano Ballesteros wins the Open.

1985   Dunhill Nations Cup instituted. Australia win.

1986   Belle Robertson wins Scottish Ladies Amateur for seventh time. Australia win Dunhill Cup.

1987   Curtis Strange sets record of 62. England win Dunhill Cup.

1988   St. Andrews Trophy. Great Britain and Ireland beat Europe 15 - 8. Ireland win Dunhill Cup.

1989   St. Andrews Links Trophy instituted. Winner Russell Claydon. U.S.A. win Dunhill Cup.

1990   S. Bouvier wins Links Trophy. Open Championship. Jack Nicklaus made honorary member of Royal and Ancient. Royal and Ancient's £1·5 million museum on Bruce Embankment opened.

Off the Tee – Fact File

1.   The Old Course is the oldest golf course in the world. Anyone can play here or on the other three courses — the New, the Eden and the Jubilee. There is also a nine hole course. You don't need to be a member of a club and you don't need an introduction.

2.   The Old Course once consisted of 22 holes — 11 out and 11 home. It started and finished more or less where Murray Park meets the Scores. Then players turned after the first 11 and playing over the same ground, holed out in the same holes. The sanddunes were then under water and the course was one third of its present width.

3.   There was once a move to fill in the Sunderland bunker, a dangerous little cavern which traps those who opt for the "safe" line at the 15th hole. But local golfers re-opened the bunker in the dead of night.

4.   All arrangements for the promotion and presentation of the Open are made by the Royal and Ancient Club each year and all profits are given to the general welfare of golf.

5.   In 1930 Bobby Jones won the Amateur and Open Championship of Britain and America in one season. On accepting the Freedom of St. Andrews many years later he said: "The more I studied the Old Course, the more I loved it and the more I loved it, the more I studied it, so that I came to feel that it was, for me, the most favourable meeting ground possible for an important contest. I felt that my knowledge of the course enabled me to play it with patience and restraint until she might exact her toll from my adversary who might treat her with less respect and understanding."

6.   The Open had been played 12 times at Prestwick before it first moved to St. Andrews in 1873. After Young Tom Morris won four Open Championships in a row it was decided that the event should be held at his course. Nowadays the Open is played on a rota basis around a short list of links courses.

7.   Early golfers over the Old Course used the featherie, a top hat of goose feathers stitched into a bull-hide skin. The first clubs were hickory shafts. In the 20th century the arrival of the rubber-cored ball and the steel shaft club have been the most significant developments.

8.   There were resignations from the Society of St. Andrews Golfers in 1814 when the annual

subscription was increased to a guinea (£1.05 pence). In those days members were elected by ballot and two black balls were sufficient to bar them. Today the procedure is for a candidate to be proposed and seconded by members. His name then goes into the candidates' book which is circulated among the membership. Proposers or objectors can register their views accordingly. Once accepted applicants go on a waiting list.

9.   The early golfers liked to relax in convivial surroundings after a round. In the 18th century they gathered once a fortnight at Baillie Glass's House, an inn which probably became the Black Bull. Dinner was a shilling and members had to pay up whether present or not. Doctor Johnson and his travelling companion Boswell dined on haddock and mutton chops at Glass's during a visit to St. Andrews in 1773.

10.   Young Tom Morris was one of St. Andrews' golfing greats and although he died at a young age, from a burst artery in the lung, those who knew and loved him believed that he really suffered a broken heart. His young wife died very suddenly in the autumn of 1875 while he was playing with his father at North Berwick. But Young Tom never recovered from the shock and died on the following Christmas Eve. The inscription on his memorial in the cathedral churchyard reads: "He thrice won the Champion belt and held it without rivalry, and yet without envy, his many amiable qualities being no less acknowledged than his golfing achievements."

Nicklaus's St. Andrews

The year 1984 saw a multitude of threads sewn into St. Andrews' rich tapestry. Most were connected with that year's Open Championship, one which will be recalled with fondness by some, heartbreak by others, delight by at least one and deep gratitude by one other.

Thanks to the commercial foresight of the enlightened Royal and Ancient Golf Club modern Open Championships are seen by millions of television viewers world-wide and journalists, magazine writers and authors give golf's oldest championship their undivided attention for at least one week every July.

The result is that the Open is now far and away the best championship in the world. It may not have the seemingly-soft gentility or garden-party atmosphere of the US Masters at Augusta each spring but it attracts a much stronger field than the Masters or the other two commonly-accepted 'major', the United States Open and the United States PGA Championship.

Quite simply however, it is not only the oldest and most important, it is the finest and when the Royal and Ancient's rota system of taking the Championship to the finest links courses in Scotland and England brings it round again to St. Andrews an extra ingredient is added.

St. Andrews Opens are always special. Those in 1970 and 1978, both won by Jack Nicklaus, were memorable for their own reasons.

The 1984 Championship exceeded them. It had a poignant link with Robert Tyre Jones Jnr., probably the finest-ever exponent of the Royal and Ancient game and unarguably the finest-ever amateur. For the Jones' life story was one which inspired a certain youngster born in Columbus, Ohio on January 21, 1940, years after Jones had retired. He was christened Jack William Nicklaus.

Young Nicklaus' father was a devoted fan of Jones who never tired of extolling the Jones' virtues both as a golfer and as gentleman to his impressionable sibling. Bobby Jones, Freeman of St. Andrews, was the boyhood hero of Jack Nicklaus and remained so until his death in 1971. By then powerhouse Nicklaus, of whom Jones once said: "Jack Nicklaus plays a game with which I am not familiar", had won two Open, two United States Opens, two United States PGA championships and three Masters Green Jackets. He was well established as the dominant figure of his era.

Yet whenever they came face to face Nicklaus had such deep respect for this hero he was never able to address him as other than "Mr. Jones." The first chapter of his book "The Greatest Game of All" is devoted to Jones and the last line of that opening chapter reads: "In a word, he (Bobby Jones) has embodied the spirit of golf."

Throughout his own spectacularly successful career Jack Nicklaus has endeavoured to attain and live up to the standards set by Mr. Jones.

Those efforts did not go unnoticed by the citizenry of St. Andrews, helped enormously of course by his Open wins of 1970 and 1978, and in 1984 the University of St. Andrews offered him the Degree of Doctor of Laws, Honoris Causa. He accepted with alacrity and humility and has graciously allowed us to reprint the speech he delivered at the Graduation Ceremony on July 17, 1984. This is it:–

‘ Vice-Chancellor, Mr. McDowall, My Lords, Ladies and Gentlemen, Faculty and Students.

I am not a person who lives much in the past, but at a time like this, it is impossible to stop the mind from overflowing with special memories. If I were to try to share with you all of those, we would be here until well into the Open Championship, which would definitely not please your neighbours across the way at the Royal and Ancient. So I am going to limit myself to just a few remarks. Please do not mistake this brevity for lack of feeling or appreciation, because I assure you what I have to say comes from my heart.

I am deeply honoured to stand before you today for many reasons, but most of all as an individual who truly appreciates the close ties between my country and St. Andrews. This close relationship stems back to James Wilson, a native son of St. Andrews and a former student at this University, who signed our Declaration of Independence. But the link that means the most to me is the close tie that was developed between the University of St. Andrews and Robert Tyre Jones Jr., a very special person in my life and an inspiration to all who had an opportunity to know him. I am extremely proud to be a Director of the Robert T. Jones Jr. Memorial Scholarship Fund established in this fine man's name to honour both his tremendous contributions to golf and to the goodwill he built between our countries. It is a pleasure for me to salute the four 1984 Jones Scholars who are here today.

I am particularly honoured to be here at one of the world's most renowned Universities. My particular participation in Higher Education came through one of America's largest universities, Ohio State. In retrospect, I learned many things at Ohio State, the chief among them being the great importance of institutions such as yours, not only in educating young people, but in helping them to achieve complete and fruitful lives as civilised members of society.

I have made my way largely in athletics and would not describe myself as an academic, although having three children attending university with two more to go should give me some academic standing. Even so, I want to congratulate everyone involved with this great and ancient university for all your effort, devotion and concern. The world has always needed you, but never more than it does today.

Although I know that the University is as international

as it is renowned, I would like to say a word or two about the country to which I am sure it has contributed the most over these past 570 years.

I first came to Scotland in 1959 to play in the Walker Cup matches, and I still cringe at the thought of the raw, crewcut, over-confident nineteen-year-old who was sure he could take apart both the Muirfield course and everyone on it without batting an eye. My love for this country began on that first trip, and it has grown stronger and deeper with each succeeding visit. Hopefully the passage of time has at least partly made up for a certain brashness during my first visit.

I love the style and the atmosphere of Scottish Golf, and the great Scottish Links and courses. I am also in constant awe of the variety and beauty of the Scottish terrain. But what has always made me love Scotland the most is the people.

Nowhere on earth have I been received more warmly, more affectionately, or with greater understanding than by the people of this country. I can assure you that the memories of my times here will never fade.

Of all my memories, the richest have come from right here, St. Andrews, this lovely city of such great lore and legend, renowned for so many qualities and achievements beyond the old and noble game we are once again celebrating this week. One thing I have learned is that there always have been, and always will be, conflicting opinions on that place across the road where shortly the world's finest players will once again be in competition for the most cherished International Golf Championship on earth. Be that as it may, it is unimaginable to me how any true golfer, anyone who really cares about the game, can fail to enjoy and appreciate St. Andrews.

I came to St. Andrews for the first time twenty years ago to play in the Open Championship of 1964, and I came back to win in 1970 and again in 1978. It was on that third visit I had the most memorable experience of my golfing life. On that last day, walking down the eighteenth fairway to my third Open Championship was a moment I will cherish forever. It is times such as that one which make us certain there is only one Home of Golf: St. Andrews. This is where the greatest game of all truly began, and where its history and tradition will remain for centuries to come.

As I have said many times before, this is my favourite place in all the golfing world. I promise you I will still be saying exactly that whatever the result next Sunday evening.

Vice-Chancellor, Mr. McDowall, members of this great institution, Lords, Ladies and Gentlemen, golfers, golf fans and friends, you have done me great honour today, and I thank you most sincerely. On behalf of Barbara and our five children, I stand before you with deep appreciation and humility, and with a fond wish for health, happiness, peace and goodwill for each of you and for the world in which we live.

Thank you. '

For all his prominence in world sport for more than twenty years Doctor Nicklaus was deeply moved by his honorary degree. So much so that a stomach upset, induced no doubt by the nervous tension and strain of his graduation, prevented him attending the Past Champions Dinner in the Royal and Ancient Club that evening. It also prevented him playing his best golf in the championship he cherishes so dearly but he did fly home to West Palm Beach a deeply grateful, if not a delighted, man nonetheless.

The most delighted person that 1984 Open Championship was the well-deserved winner Severiano Ballesteros.

The Spaniard had arrived at the Home of Golf at odds with his game, often the most devastating and exciting since the hey-day of Royal and Ancient Honorary Member

Arnold Palmer. A few quiet words of advice on the eve of
the Championship however from Brazilian professional
Jaime Gonzales and Argentinian Vicente Fernandez
(winner of the 1979 Colgate over the Old Course) saw
Seve in a much more settled frame of mind.

As a man with a deep love and appreciation for the
history of golf he was desperate to succeed, particularly
as his mother Carmen and fiancee, also Carmen, were
with him that week.

Young Australian Ian Baker Finch led for most of the
four days but in the end it was the experience, flair and
golfing genius of Ballesteros which won the day, helped
by a totally uncharacteristic lapse by America's Tom
Watson. The man from Kansas City had already annexed
golf's oldest title five times and was understandably
eager to match Harry Vardon's record of six, particularly
at the Home of Golf.

On the 17th tee, the 71st hole of the Championship,
Watson stood at eleven under par, just as Ballesteros had
done a few minutes earlier. Watson drove long and well,
although for a heart-stopping moment he feared he
might have driven out of bounds into the grounds of the
Old Course Golf and Country Club.

Then came the crucial moment. The time of decision.
What club to hit to the notorious Road Hole green,
graveyard of so many hopes down the centuries? Watson
was not to know that up ahead Ballesteros had driven
into rough on the left of the fairway before hitting the
putting surface with a six iron. The American elected to
hit a two-iron. It was always too strong. The shot cleared
the green and the ball bounced on the road, then the wall
before coming to rest on a small patch of grass. He
needed a miracle. None was forthcoming and his five at
the par four hole was achieved seconds after Ballesteros
had holed a birdie putt in the amphitheatre created by the
grandstands round the last green.

The Spaniard's joy was unbridled. Watson's despair

etched deeply on his face. The American then had to hole out for an eagle two at the 18th to force a play-off but that was beyond him. Down the centuries that 18th green has witnessed many moments of happiness but surely none more gleefully uninhibited than Seve's paso double of delight. He had predicted the previous evening that if he could par the 17th hole in the final round he would become Open Champion 1984. Severiano the Prophet was proved right.

The Old Lady Has A New Suitor

Golf's World Cup was founded in 1953 as an international team event for professional golfers with the laudable intent of spreading international goodwill. In the early 1980's it began to flounder as more and more international stars declined invitations to compete. Various reasons and excuses were proffered but it seems likely that money, that root of all evil, was behind most of the polite 'No thank you' notes. There was no cash for representing your country in the World Cup, only honour.

In 1985 Mark Hume McCormack's International Management Group came up with an alternative. A Nations Cup with a prize fund of $1 million was instituted under the sponsorship of Alfred Dunhill, manufacturers and purveyors of quality clothing, watches and accessories. It was the richest team event in golf with the major nations pitting their power against emerging countries such as Nigeria and the venue of course was the Old Course – in autumn. Wise, and not so wise, shook their heads and muttered darkly that St. Andrews at that time of year would have ferocious weather, that the Dunhill

Cup was a non-starter doomed to failure.

However the golfing gods smiled on McCormack and the Dunhill Nations Cup that first year and the three-man Australian side which triumphed. The Aussies, led by Greg Norman, won the first two Dunhills in fact. Then came 1987.

As Europe had recorded their first-ever Ryder Cup triumph on American soil the previous week at US Captain Jack Nicklaus' very own Muirfield Village Club, no less, and Scotland's team was Sandy Lyle, Sam Torrance and Gordon Brand Jnr., – all of whom had played their part in Columbus, Ohio, – a home win was expected. The three Scots even paraded in full Highland Dress on the eve of the tournament and promised to wear the kilt again at the victory dinner.

Alas, the headlines were not to be theirs with England's Nick Faldo, Howard Clark and the 'other' Gordon Brand beating them 2 -1 in the final of the medal match play format, a final overshadowed by the finest golf ever played on the Old Course.

In the second round Rodger Davis of Australia met Canadian Don Halldorson and broke Neil Coles' 27 year old course record of 65 with a nine under par 63. Coles' record had in fact been equalled by Nick Faldo in the 1979 PGA Championship and by Norman and Davis himself in previous Dunhill Nations Cup matches. Rodger, always nattily attired in Plus-Fours and monogramed hose, had seven threes, a two and ten fours in his remarkable 63. His record did not last for long however, even although the sponsors were so confident it would they presented him with a watch.

On the final day Australia and the United States battled it out for third and fourth places behind England and Scotland with Norman, unbeaten in 11 Dunhill Cup ties, facing Curtis Strange.

Norman shot a 70 that calm Sunday afternoon – and lost by no fewer than eight strokes as the Virginian played consummate golf on a course with superb greens made receptive by rain.

His round of 62 deserves, indeed demands, recording in detail. This was it:

First hole: Driver, sand wedge, 18 foot putt. Birdie three.
Second hole: Driver, eight iron, two putts from 14 feet. Par four.
Third hole: Driver, wedge, seven foot putt. Birdie three.
Fourth hole: Driver, four iron, two putts from 28 feet. Par four.
Fifth hole: Driver, five wood, three putts from 80 feet. Par five.
Sixth hole: Driver, sand wedge, two putts from 26 feet. Par four.
Seventh hole: Driver, sand wedge, five inch putt. Birdie three.
Eighth hole: Five iron, 16 foot putt. Birdie two.
Ninth hole: Driver, nine iron, 12 foot putt. Birdie three.
OUT IN 31.

Tenth hole: Driver, sand wedge, 4 foot putt. Birdie three.
Eleventh hole: Seven iron, 15 foot putt. Birdie two.
Twelfth hole: Driver, wedge, 25 foot putt. Birdie two.
Thirteenth hole: Driver, two iron, two putts from 80 feet. Par four.
Fourteenth hole: Driver, three iron, five iron, two putts from 28 feet. Par five.
Fifteenth hole: Driver, five iron, 16 foot putt. Birdie three.
Sixteenth hole: Driver, seven iron, two putts from 14 feet. Par four.
Seventeenth hole: Driver, four iron, two putts from 72 feet. Par four.
Eighteenth hole: Driver, wedge, 14 foot putt. Birdie three.
HOME IN 31 – TOTAL 62.

The vanquished Norman was the very essence of sportsmanship, as ever, when he said admiringly: "It was great just to see such a round at close quarters. If you have to lose let it be to a 62 on the Old Course."

The Dunhill Nations Cup is now a firm fixture on the St. Andrews golfing calendar.

Just as 1984 was a momentous year at St. Andrews so was 1990 when the Open returned. Jack Nicklaus, honoured by the University in 1984, was made an honorary member of the Royal and Ancient who, after many years, finally opened a magnificent new museum by the Bruce Embankment for their Tutenkhamun-like trove of golfing treasures. They invited all past champions to donate something to the museum and Doug Sanders immediately offered the putter with which he missed 'that putt' to lose to Nicklaus in 1970.

Arnold Palmer presented a one iron, 1951 champion Max Faulkner a pair of his gaudy trousers and Tom Weiskopf the clubs he used to win so majestically at Troon in 1973.

Despite its antiquity and world-renown as the repository of all that is historic in golf, St. Andrews refuses to stand still and risk being by-passed as the 21st century looms.

The go-ahead Links Management Committee had the Jubilee Course re-designed and strengthened by Donald Steel and course-record holder Curtis Strange officially opened it in 1989.

At the time of writing the Eden Course was being re-modelled, and plans for new changing rooms and another 18-hole course, the Strathtyrum, were on the stocks.

In keeping with their image of custodians of the game of golf the Royal and Ancient bought a share of the Old Course Golf and Country Club when it was sold by Frank Sheridan in 1989 and they now have guaranteed five-star accommodation for the the world's finest golfers when they visit St. Andrews, Home of Golf.

Humour – off the Tee

In 1983 Australian golfer Jack Newton, runner-up to Severiano Ballesteros in the 1980 US Masters at Augusta, had an horrific accident when he was almost ripped in two by the propellor of a private plane. His injuries were dreadful and he came close to losing his life. However "Newt the Beaut." is made of stern stuff and he travelled to St. Andrews in 1984 to see old friends, pay his tributes to the home of Golf, and do some television commentary. Jack has always liked to relax of an evening and one night in the Auld Grey Toon he had quite a few drams. Come time to go home he called a local taxi company and asked for a car to take him back to his hotel. When the voice at the other end of the line asked where he was

Jack replied: "I've no idea, mate. But I won't be hard to find. I am the only one-eyed, one-armed drunk Australian golfer in St. Andrews." The taxi driver found him!

The young minister, from a parish not many miles from St. Andrews, was beaten by an elderly parishioner. Seeing a look of depression on the cleric's face the winner declared: "Cheer up, you'll win at the finish when you eventually bury me one day." That's all very well", said the minister, "But it will still be your hole!"

What is a handicapped golfer?
One who plays with the boss!

Heard at the 19th: My wife is going to leave if I don't give up the game.

I say, that's tough old boy.

True enough, I'll certainly miss her!

Touts were selling Open tickets for £50.00 each but Jamie declined their approach, saying he would sooner spend the money on a woman.

"OK, if that's what you want," said the tout, "But with this ticket you get 18 holes."

The fed-up caddie couldn't resist it when the veteran said he'd move heaven and earth to break 100 on the Old Course.

"Try heaven," said the caddie, "You've already shifted most of the earth."

Parting Shot . . . . .
Why is it we blame fate for most accidents but take personal responsibility when we get a hole in one?

Old Course – Hole by Hole

All the world's best players - and countless thousands of the worst - have played the revered Old Course. Many, such as the legendary Bobby Jones, hated it at first sight but in time grew to love it more dearly than any other. With its vast double greens, unique in championship golf, putting can be even more important on the Old Course than anywhere else.

This is a guide from the first to the 18th.

Hole One. 370 yards. Par Four. Burn.

A benign looking hole from the tee with first and 18th fairways sharing the same huge expanse of inviting green grass. The trouble is in the shape of the Swilcan Burn which snakes its way across in front of the green. Nevertheless it is not the most demanding of starts.

Hole two. 411 yards. Par Four. Dyke.

Like most holes on the Old a good drive is essential here. As ever the easy option is to play left away from the trouble but Cheape's Bunker lies in wait at the Dyke with the most rewarding line up the right, skirting the whins.

Hole Three. 371 yards. Par Four. Cartgate Out.

Good birdie chance. Once again there is plenty room to drive the ball up the left but the right hand side, despite a rash of small bunkers, will favour the bold. The green has many, not always apparent, swings and borrows.

Hole Four. 463 Yards. Par Four. Ginger Beer.

A difficult hole by any standards but at least offering three driving options. Once more the best is down the right, the narrow side, avoiding a huge tract of hilly rough just to the left of centre. Or you can go away left to a plateau and the 15th fairway. Third choice is for the big hitter to carry the rough - and run the risk of Cottage Bunker. The approach has to negotiate a big mound in front of the green.

Hole Five. 564 yards. Par Five. Hole o'Cross.

The drive here must be left to avoid a nasty nest of bunkers cutting into the right hand side of the fairway which gather any shot not properly positioned from the tee. Long hitters can reach the green in two, there is a pair of bunkers cut in to the hill fronting the green.

Hole Six. 416 yards. Par Four. Heathery Out.

Blind tee shot but one of the more straightforward holes because there are clear indications of the safe line to take. However be wary of going too far left and finding the ball buried in the Coffin bunkers.

Hole Seven. 372 Yards. Par Four. High Out.

This hole plays as a dog leg left to right and a good drive is needed to reach the flat portion of the fairway which the 7th shares with the 11th. The green is guarded by Shell Bunker and a sharp escarpment which calls for a deft touch with the approach.

Hole Eight. 178 Yards. Par Three. Short.

First of the par threes and the green nestles behind a mound which holes the Short Hole Bunker. Looks easy but can be most deceptive. Proper club selection is the key.

Hole Nine. 356 Yards. Par Four. End.

The 9th is part of the famous Loop - which starts at the 7th and ends at the 11th - where scores can be made or wrecked. This hole can often be in reach from the tee with only heather on the left and Boase's Bunker guarding the straight line. The second shot is rarely more than a short pitch or chip.

Hole Ten. 342 Yards. Par Four. Bobby Jones.

Named after the great American Freeman of St. Andrews this hole, like the previous one, can be reached from the tee in the proper conditions. Yet there is trouble aplenty for the unwary. Whins and heather abound on the left and undulating, rising ground in front of the green has to be negotiated.

Hole Eleven. 172 Yards. Par Three. High In.

One of the greatest short holes in golf and one frequently copied by course designers. Mere distance often means little. The strengths of this hole are the wind, the steeply sloping green, Hill Bunker and Shell Bunker. Bobby Jones hit his tee shot into Hill Bunker on his first visit then tore up his card. Legend had it that Jones finally hit his ball into the Eden Estuary behind the green in anger. He later denied that however, insisting he never got his ball out of the bunker!

Hole 12. 316 Yards. Par Four. Heathery In.

One of golf's great sucker holes. Standing on the tee there is no hint of trouble as the player looks towards the beckoning green. But there is trouble galore in the shape of nasty little bunkers hidden in folds in the ground in the middle of the fairway. The drive must be right to set up the approach to what is little more than a narrow shelf of a green.

Hole 13. 425 Yards. Par Four. Hole o' Cross In.

This hole demands cautious treatment from the tee. The coffins bunkers lie in wait just off the left of the fairway but too tight a line to avoid those leaves a blind second shot to a vast double green. Well left with the drive is the safe route offering a view of the green over Cat's Trap and Lion's Mouth bunkers.

Hole 14. 567 Yards. Par Five. Long.

From the tee the out of bounds wall on the right is clearly visible as are the dreaded bunkers called The Beardies down the left. Once those hurdles are negotiated the cavernous Hell Bunker lies in wait for a less-than-perfect approach to a fiendishly difficult green.

Hole 15. 413 Yards. Par Four. Cartgate In.

Not one of the most testing pars - if a long straight drive is struck. But the second has to be played with delicacy to get anywhere near the hole which is normally on the lower section of the putting surface.

Hole 16. 382 Yards. Par Four. Corner of the Dyke.

The out of bounds fence down the right spells danger with the Principal's Nose bunker, followed by Deacon Syme, just waiting to trap tee shots hit a fraction off line. Best to go well left, leaving a longer approach.

Hole 17. 461 Yards. Par Four. Road.

Probably the finest par four in golf and certainly the most notorious. A dog leg left to right it calls for a bold drive over the corner of the sheds at the Old Course Hotel. Too far right, however, and you are out of bounds. The second can easily run on to the road behind the green which gives the hole its name. This hole has been the graveyard of many hopes including those of Tom Watson whose two iron on to the Road cost him the 1984 Open.

Hole 18. 354 Yards. Par Four. Tom Morris.

Like the first, with which it shares an enormous fairway, this looks no problem at all. You can drive it anywhere except right with out of bounds all the way over the white fence. In fact in the 1970 Open Jack Nicklaus tore off his sweater and drove the green en route to his victory over Doug Sanders who finally missed a short putt for victory then lost the play-off. For those without the power of Nicklaus however the approach to a vast green which slopes back to front and right to left can pose problems for there is the notorious Valley of Sin to be negotiated. The choice whether to pitch to the flag with a lofted club or go for a canny Scottish chip and run is for the player to make. Nick Faldo chose the latter in 1990, holed for an eagle two and went on to win the Open Championship.

At the nineteenth . . .

The Open returned to St. Andrews in 1990 with a record entry for the 119th Championship. A massive total of 1707 hopefuls sent in entry forms, exceeding the previous record of 1481 at Royal Troon in 1989 and almost 300 more than the previous highest, at St. Andrews in 1984. The attraction of playing in an Open at the Home of Golf drew the exceptional entry and forced the Royal and Ancient to add South Herts Golf Club to the original list of seven Regional Qualifying courses and include Panmure Golf Club at Barry near Carnoustie as a fifth Final Qualifying course.

Said R and A secretary Michael Bonallack: "The quality, even more than the record entry, again underlines the Open as the world's number one Championship and St. Andrews as the Home of Golf."

The entries included 471 players from 30 countries outwith Great Britain and Ireland. No fewer than 47 of the top in the Sony World Rankings filed entry forms.

At the nineteenth . . .